DATE			
JUL 7 '78			
SEP 1 2 1989			
MAR 0 2 '92			
APR 1 4 '92			
OCT 2 0 '92			
APR 2 5 1995			
NOV 0 2 1999			

*31 Letters
and 13 Dreams*

By Richard Hugo

31 Letters
and 13 Dreams

~~~~~~~~~~~~~~~~~~~~

Poems by Richard Hugo

W · W · NORTON & COMPANY · INC ·
NEW YORK

Some of these poems have appeared in the following publications.

American Review (formerly *New American Review*), *The Atlantic Monthly*, *boundary 2*, *Chicago Review*, *Colorado State Review*, *The Iowa Review*, *The New York Quarterly*, *Periphery*, *Quarry* (now *Quarry West*), *Seizure*, and *Southwest Review*.

"Letter to Wagoner from Port Townsend," "Letter to Welch from Browning," "Letter to Logan from Milltown," "Letter to Levertov from Butte," "Letter to Scanlon from White-hall," and "Letter to Bell from Missoula" appeared in *The American Poetry Review* and were reprinted in *The New Naked Poetry*, an anthology edited by Stephen Berg and Robert Mazey, which also included "Letter to Reed from Lolo," first printed in *Ironwood*. "Letter to Wagoner from Port Townsend" also appeared in the author's book, *Rain Five Days and I Love It*. "Letter to Gale from Ovando," "Letter to Hill from St. Ignatius," "Letter to Blessing from Missoula," "Letter to Oberg from Pony," "Letter to Goldbarth from Big Fork," "Letter to Haislip from Hot Springs," "Letter to Birch from Deer Lodge," "Letter to Libbey from St. Regis," "In Your Dream after Falling in Love," "In Your Racing Dream," "Letter to Sister Madeline from Iowa City," "Letter to Hanson from Miami," "Letter to Ammons from Maratea," "Letter to Snyder from Montana," "In Your Big Dream," and "In Your Small Dream" originally appeared in *The American Poetry Review*. "Note to R. H. from Strongs-ville" first appeared in *Antaeus*. "Letter to Matthews from Barton Street Flats" was first printed in the *Graham House Review*. "In Your Fugitive Dream" was titled "Fugitive" when it appeared in *The Ohio Review*. "In Your Blue Dream" was first published in *Poetry*. "In Your Bad Dream" and "Letter to Peterson from the Pike Place Market" were originally published in *Poetry Northwest*.

First Edition

Library of Congress Cataloging in Publication Data

Hugo, Richard F
    31 letters and 13 dreams.

    I. Title.
PS3515.U3T5   811'.5'4   77–22156
ISBN 0-393-04481-5
ISBN 0-393-04490-4 pbk.

1 2 3 4 5 6 7 8 9 0

In Memory

Arthur Oberg   1938–1977

"It is not love is second best, but all.
Before, after words. Loving words.
And in that order."

Contents

*31 Letters
and 13 Dreams*

Letter to Kizer from Seattle

Dear Condor: Much thanks for that telephonic support
from North Carolina when I suddenly went ape
in the Iowa tulips. Lord, but I'm ashamed.
I was afraid, it seemed, according to the doctor
of impending success, winning some poetry prizes
or getting a wet kiss. The more popular I got,
the softer the soft cry in my head: Don't believe them.
You were never good. Then I broke and proved it.
Ten successive days I alienated women
I liked best. I told a coed why her poems were bad
(they weren't) and didn't understand a word I said.
Really warped. The phrase "I'll be all right"
came out too many unsolicited times. I'm o.k. now.
I'm back at the primal source of poems: wind, sea
and rain, the market and the salmon. Speaking
of the market, they're having a vital election here.
Save the market? Tear it down? The forces of evil
maintain they're trying to save it too, obscuring,
of course, the issue. The forces of righteousness,
me and my friends, are praying for a storm, one
of those grim dark rolling southwest downpours
that will leave the electorate sane. I'm the last poet
to teach the Roethke chair under Heilman.
He's retiring after 23 years. Most of the old gang
is gone. Sol Katz is aging. Who isn't? It's close now
to the end of summer and would you believe it
I've ignored the Blue Moon. I did go to White Center,
you know, my home town, and the people there,
many are the same, but also aging, balding, remarkably
polite and calm. A man whose name escapes me
said he thinks he had known me, the boy who went alone

3

to Longfellow Creek and who laughed and cried
for no reason. The city is huge, maybe three quarters
of a million and lots of crime. They are indicting
the former chief of police. Sorry to be so rambling.
I eat lunch with J. Hillis Miller, brilliant and nice
as they come, in the faculty club, overlooking the lake,
much of it now filled in. And I tour old haunts,
been twice to Kapowsin. One trout. One perch. One poem.
Take care, oh wisest of condors. Love. Dick. Thanks again.

Letter to Bell from Missoula

Dear Marvin: Months since I left broke down and sobbing
in the parking lot, grateful for the depth
of your understanding and since then I've been treated
in Seattle and I'm in control like Genghis Khan.
That was a hairy one, the drive west, my nerves so strung
I couldn't sign a recognizable name on credit slips.
And those station attendants' looks. Until Sheridan
I took the most degenerate motels I saw because they seemed
to be where I belonged. I found my way by instinct
to bad restaurants and managed to degrade myself
in front of waitresses so dumb I damn near offered them
lessons in expression of disdain. Now, it's all a blur.
Iowa. South Dakota. Wyoming. Lots of troublesome déja vu
in towns I'd seen or never seen before. It's snowing
in Missoula, has been off and on for days but no fierce winds
and no regrets. I'm living alone in a house I bought,
last payment due 2001. Yesterday, a religious nut
came to the door and offered me unqualified salvation
if I took a year's subscription to Essential Sun Beam.
I told him I was Taoist and he went away. Today,
a funny dog, half dachshund, waddles through my yard.
A neighbor boy, Bud, poor, shovels my walk for a dollar
and on the radio a break is predicted. A voice is saying,
periods of sun tomorrow, a high front from the coast.
For no reason, I keep remembering my first woman
and how I said afterward happy, so that's what you do.
I think of you and Dorothy. Stay healthy. Love. Dick.

Letter to Sister Madeline from Iowa City

Dear Madeline: I'm getting strange when I drink. In Solon
I take a booth alone in the back and play old tunes
on the juke box, trying, I suppose, to feel some way
I felt when I was young. But things keep breaking in.
For instance, last night they had a live band and single
women from surrounding farms kept asking me to dance.
I wanted them to go away. I'm drunk, I said. I don't know
how to dance, and kept trying to remember every time
a woman did me wrong. I wanted to scream at the women,
leave me alone. Can't you see, I'm rotten. Go dance
with decent farm hands. I don't remember dancing
but I know I danced. Outside of these odd moments
I am doing well. Marvin Bell is fun to work with. The load
is light. No complaints except for weather. In the west
where we have mountains, we can always assume that hidden
from us but coming is something better. Here, no illusion.
The weather, seldom good, goes on forever. It covers
a dozen states. For instance, if it's lousy like usual
in Cincinnati, it is equally lousy here in Iowa City.
That's what's getting me down. At night in my trailer home
I drink alone into the early hours listening to Chicago
on the radio, a sentimental all night station. Last night
they featured Benny Goodman. And I think over and over
of a hundred rejections at the hands of merciless women.
And of women leaving. I think some days I should be like you
and embrace a religion, and hope to create for myself
a definite stance that keeps people away while I keep looking
for my real disposition, and not go to bed starving like I do,
bitter and plotting revenge. I have a plan, not serious,
for killing myself and leaving behind a beautiful note

6

in red paint on the ceiling, worded so the words would crawl
in the ears of women I have known like an ultrasonic hum.
And they would go mad, my life forever on their hands,
my words forever in their brains. The trouble with that plan—
they don't print the contents of suicide notes in the papers.
A conspiracy to discourage poets and drunks. And besides,
I happen to like Benny Goodman and booze, and maybe
tomorrow they'll play him again. A report says in Cincinnati
it's clearing. About time. Five A.M., and I'm wobbling off
to a dream of sea nymphs issued by the sea. Love always. Dick.

In Your Fugitive Dream

Though Tuesday, 11 A.M., the shops are locked.
You try the meat store. Only the muffled buzz
of a fly inside. You rattle the glass
of the drugstore, yelling "I have a prescription."
A 40-watt bulb burns over the soda fountain.
You think, when you find no one around, if really
the town is empty, wind should be blowing.
Sun presses the buildings down. Birds
on the street seem to be resting enroute.
You break into a dress shop and imagine women
you've had in clothes the manikins wear.
You rip a dress from a plaster figure and roar.
The way you yell "rape" it echoes about
the streets and comes back "hope" as it dies.
You find whiskey in the bar. You answer
your order with "Yes, sir. Coming right up."
When they find you the whole bar is laughing.
Men tell the police, "That guy's o.k.
Leave him alone," and the cop in charge grins.
You watch them search your luggage. Then
you remember what you carry and start to explain.

Letter to Simic from Boulder

Dear Charles: And so we meet once in San Francisco and I
learn I bombed you long ago in Belgrade when you were five.
I remember. We were after a bridge on the Danube
hoping to cut the German armies off as they fled north
from Greece. We missed. Not unusual, considering I
was one of the bombardiers. I couldn't hit my ass if
I sat on the Norden or rode a bomb down singing
The Star Spangled Banner. I remember Belgrade opened
like a rose when we came in. Not much flak. I didn't know
about the daily hangings, the 80,000 Slavs who dangled
from German ropes in the city, lessons to the rest.
I was interested mainly in staying alive, that moment
the plane jumped free from the weight of bombs and we went home.
What did you speak then? Serb, I suppose. And what did your mind
do with the terrible howl of bombs? What is Serb for "fear"?
It must be the same as in English, one long primitive wail
of dying children, one child fixed forever in dead stare.
I don't apologize for the war, or what I was. I was
willingly confused by the times. I think I even believed
in heroics (for others, not for me). I believed the necessity
of that suffering world, hoping it would learn not to do
it again. But I was young. The world never learns. History
has a way of making the past palatable, the dead
a dream. Dear Charles, I'm glad you avoided the bombs, that you
live with us now and write poems. I must tell you though,
I felt funny that day in San Francisco. I kept saying
to myself, he was one on the ground that day, the sky
eerie mustard and our engines roaring everything
out of the way. And the world comes clean in moments
like that for survivors. The world comes clean as clouds
in summer, the pure puffed white, soft birds careening

9

in and out, our lives with a chance to drift on slow
over the world, our bomb bays empty, the target forgotten,
the enemy ignored. Nice to meet you finally after
all that mindless hate. Next time, if you want to be sure
you survive, sit on the bridge I'm trying to hit and wave.
I'm coming in on course but nervous and my cross hairs flutter.
Wherever you are on earth, you are safe. I'm aiming but
my bombs are candy and I've lost the lead plane. Your friend, Dick.

Letter to Matthews from Barton Street Flats

Dear Bill: This is where the Nisei farmed, here where the blacktop
of a vast shopping complex covers the rich black bottom land.
Lettuce sparkled like a lake. Then, the war took everything,
farm, farmers and my faith that change (I really mean loss)
is paced slow enough for the blood to adjust. I believed
the detention of Tada, my friend, was temporary madness
like the war. Someday, I thought, it will all be over, this
tearing out everything, this shifting people away like
so many pigs to single thickness walled shacks in Wyoming
where winter rips like the insane self-righteous tongue
of the times. In Germany, Jews. In America, Japs.
They came back and their property was gone, some technicality
those guardians of society, lawyers found. Or their goods
had burned in unexplained fires. Tada came back wounded
from honest German guns and got insulted in White Center—
I was with him—oh, a dreadful scene. He moved justly bitter
to Milwaukee. Haven't seen him in years. Why do I think
of this today? Why, faced with this supermarket parking lot
filled with gleaming new cars, people shopping unaware
a creek runs under them, do I think back thirty some years
to that time all change began, never to stop, not even
to slow down one moment for us to study our loss, to recall
the Japanese farmers bent deep to the soil? Hell, Bill,
I don't know. You know the mind, how it comes on the scene again
and makes tiny histories of things. And the imagination
how it wants everything back one more time, how it detests
all progress but its own, all war but the one it fights over
and over, the one no one dares win. And we can deport those
others and feel safe for a time, but old dangers (and pleasures)
return. And we return to the field of first games where,

11

when we find it again, we look hard for the broken toy,
the rock we called home plate, evidence to support our claim
our lives really happened. You can say this all better.
Please do. Write it the way it should sound. The gain will be mine.
Use my Montana address. I'm going back home, not bent
under the load of old crops, still fat and erect, still with faith
we process what grows to the end, the poem. Your good friend, Dick.

In Your War Dream

You must fly your 35 missions again.
The old base is reopened. The food is still bad.
You are disturbed. The phlegm you choked up
mornings in fear returns. You strangle on the phlegm.
You ask, "Why must I do this again?" A man
replies, "Home." You fly over one country
after another. The nations are bright like a map.
You pass over the red one. The orange one ahead
looks cold. The purple one north of that is the one
you must bomb. A wild land. Austere. The city
below seems ancient. You are on the ground.
Lovers are inside a cabin. You ask to come in.
They say "No. Keep watch on Stark Yellow Lake."
You stand beside the odd water. A terrible wind
keeps knocking you down. "I'm keeping watch
on the lake," you yell at the cabin. The lovers
don't answer. You break into the cabin. Inside
old women bake bread. They yell, "Return to the base."
You must fly your 35 missions again.

Letter to Ammons from Maratea

Dear Archie: I hope the boat trip home wasn't long
but isn't any trip on the United States line? I'm trying
a bomber crash poem and I'm working in short lines.
I wish you were here to advise me on the timing.
You time them well. I'm lost without that harsh, often
too booming voice across the page. It snowed last night
in the mountains and I consider that un-Italian.
What a bust Italy was for you. Remember when someone
asked you what you'd do in Rome, you said, walk along
the Tiber and look at weeds. You should have come here.
Phyllis speaks Italian and you'd have gotten along.
The people here are honest and the setting—Lord, the rise
of stone mountains out of the sea and the sea clearer
than gin. When it storms, the sea is blue milk
and you can look at the little things, not just weeds
but the old sepia prints of dead men ringed with flowers
and the short silver fish they catch in the Mediterranean.
Like Corson's Inlet, it says, I say, come. I hope
Richard Howard accepts your invitation to spend time
with you and Phyllis on the ocean. What good company
he is, except he seldom is because he's always working.
The only bad thing here is, I'm lonely. For three months
I haven't spoken English to anyone, and my Italian
gets by only because the Italians are *simpatici*.
I'm wrapping up the book and going soon to London.
I've sent Richard the poems and the table of contents
and he says, that's it. What better guarantee?
I'll take the train, like the man in one of my poems.
I think I'll never see this again. But then I found it
like we find all things, by lucky accident, sometimes
not so lucky, and I'll carry it with me like a man

carries a dream of curved giant women who say, come
and beckon to us, come, and who are never there
and never go away. Your Neapolitan buddy. Dick.

Letter to Hanson from Miami

Caro Mimo mio: My first trip south. It's not what
I'd expected. Flat all over, a dull placidity of sun, sky,
water, and a nagging feeling nothing is going on.
I went fishing in a barren ocean and I had some Vodka
in a bar with Donald Drummond, who is also wondering
what we're doing here. Fact is, I'm awfully frightened
and I don't know why. I keep feeling revolutionary
but I have no cause. I feel I am going to dynamite
the swimming pool. What have I got against the pool?
Or for that matter, the hotel? It must be the plane trip
down, my fear, still there, of flying, and the heavy drinking
I've been doing. The palm trees never stir. The air here
hovers in the air. I also feel the Cuban refugee waiter
hates me in the bar. Drummond, who is fine, gives me
a kind of strength. He's one of the last no bullshit men
left in the world. Don Justice is here but I haven't seen him.
I'm not sure I've seen anyone but Drummond. Though yesterday
I seem to remember I gave a reading, and on the fishing boat
this morning, was it yesterday, I had a civil conversation
with a good looking woman from Boston. I think I know
the reason I want to plant explosions. It's the same reason
I like an occasional mark of punctuation. A comma
between bears and a colon following alligator jaws.
Because I want a mark in time. I want to say: I was this,
then wham, do some awful thing and after say, now that
is what I am, and read the amazed looks on the faces
of friends. Would they line up and salute me on my way
to prison? The trouble with dramatic things, they die.
Charles A. Lindbergh. Wrong Way Corrigan. Sacco-Vanzetti.
So I do nothing. I become a passive part of the passive
Miami day, a long day, eternal maybe, and Drummond

is going back to Missouri, leaving me alone high over
the pool I'll never bomb, in the hotel I'll never bomb,
oblivious, happy. And it just struck me I'm as far from home
as I can get in the United States, a long diagonal line
across the country, and the wind that brings gray rainclouds
rolling home. Ci vediamo. L'altro Mimo. C'iao.

In Your Bad Dream

Morning at nine, seven ultra-masculine men
explain the bars of your cage are silver
in honor of our emperor. They finger the bars
and hum. Two animals, too far to name,
are fighting. One, you are certain, is destined
to win, the yellow one, the one who from here
seems shaped like a man. Your breakfast
is snake but the guard insists eel. You say hell
I've done nothing. Surely that's not a crime.
You say it and say it. When men leave, their hum
hangs thick in the air as scorn. Your car's
locked in reverse and running. The ignition
is frozen, accelerator stuck, brake shot.
You go faster and faster back. You wait for the crash.
On a bleak beach you find a piano the tide
has stranded. You hit it with a hatchet.
You crack it. You hit it again and music
rolls dissonant over the sand. You hit it
and hit it driving the weird music from it.
A dolphin is romping. He doesn't approve.
On a clean street you join the parade. Women
line the streets and applaud, but only the band.
You ask to borrow a horn and join in.
The bandmaster says we know you can't play.
You are embarrassed. You pound your chest
and yell meat. The women weave into the dark
that is forming, each to her home. You know
they don't hear your sobbing crawling the street
of this medieval town. You promise money
if they'll fire the king. You scream a last promise—
Anything. Anything. Ridicule my arm.

18

Letter to Annick from Boulder

Dear An: This will be your first widow Christmas. Such a young
death, Dave's. A rotten cheat. The thirty or forty years
he had coming torn way. I couldn't say at his grave where
we stood bowed, ignored by the freeway above us how
unlucky he was that he couldn't poke the corners of his life
and have fun. It was too grim, that's all. Too something damaged
to be anything but run from. To law. To literature. To film.
And he ran beautiful but not far enough. Forget that.
The beautiful never go far. They wait beside roads when we come back
from petty fresh triumph, holding our trophy, the head
of a lover high in a mock blood offering to the moon.
They remind us, like he did, word and not so often deed, of limits,
of the finite returned, clouds closed to end day at five P.M.,
sunset scheduled for six. I can't lose your pain, the sound
of your sobbing over the phone, the disbelief that this, this is done.
It is done, dear An. It is lousy and never over, but done
and you're in Spokane, making the movies he would have loved
about Indians, the tribes in decay and the tribes triumphant
in some vision that matters, some picture of waters and sand,
of lost sons returned bearing the scars of the green wind they sing
in that other country, the forbidden plain, the exact spot
dark blue rain ends and coyote goes free, no bounty from
this meridian on. But I get wilder than tribes and their tales.
This is the bad time, Christmas, and the myths are honed fine.
I don't believe in them but I do believe a part of us
passes above us, preoccupied on the freeway, the rest
below grieving at the grave. And that part passing oblivious west
was once the part in the cemetery, ignores and knows
what the heart is called on to absorb and reject and still pound
like an Indian drum or the ocean, to reach
by sound or in person the other, the greased final day

of the coyote, the curtain, the moment success and failure
make no matter. And it makes no matter whether we cringe
inside or roar defiance at stars. We touch each other
and ourselves no special day, no designated season,
just now and then, in a just poem under an unjust sky.
God, I get windy. This poem, any season, for you always. Dick.

Letter to Mantsch from Havre

Dear Mike: We didn't have a chance. Our starter had no change
and second base had not been plugged since early in July.
How this town turned out opening night of the tournament
to watch their Valley Furniture team wipe us, the No-
Name Tavern of Missoula, out. Remember Monty Holden,
ace Havre pitcher, barber, hero of the Highline, and his
tricky "catch-this" windup? First inning, when you hit that shot,
one on, the stands went stone. It still rockets the night.
I imagine it climbing today, somewhere in the universe,
lovelier than a girl climbs on a horse and lovelier than star.
We lost that game. No matter. Won another. Lost again
and went back talking fondly of your four home runs,
triple and single in three games, glowing in the record book.
I came back after poems. They ask me today, here in Havre,
who's that player you brought here years ago, the hitter?
So few of us are good at what we do, and what we do,
well done or not, seems futile. I'm trying to find Monty
Holden's barber shop. I want to tell him style in anything,
pitching, hitting, cutting hair, is worth our trying even
if we fail. And when that style, the graceful compact swing
leaves the home crowd hearing its blood and the ball roars off
in night like determined moon, it is our pleasure
to care about something well done. If he doesn't understand
more than the final score, if he says, "After all, we won,"
I'll know my hair will not look right after he's done,
what little hair I have, what little time. And I'll drive home
knowing his windup was all show, glad I was there years back,
that I was lucky enough to be there when with one swing
you said to all of us, this is how it's done. The ball jumps
from your bat over and over. I want my poems to jump

like that. All poems. I want to say once to a world that feels
with reason it has little chance, well done. That's the lie
I cannot shout loud as this local truth: Well done, Mike. Dick.

In Your Young Dream

You are traveling to play basketball. Your team's
a good one, boys you knew when you were young.
A game's in Wyoming, a small town, a gym
in a grammar school. You go in to practice.
No nets on the hoops. You say to the coach,
a small man, mean face, "We need nets on the rims."
He sneers as if you want luxury. You explain
how this way you can't see the shots go in.
You and another player, vaguely seen, go out
to buy nets. A neon sign on a local tavern
gives directions to the next town, a town
a woman you loved lives in. You go to your room
to phone her, to tell her you're here just
one town away to play ball. She's already
waiting in your room surrounded by children.
She says, "I'll come watch you play ball."
Though young in the dream you know you are old.
You are troubled. You know you need nets on the rims.

Letter to Reed from Lolo

Dear J. D.: One should think of Chief Joseph here, coming soft
out of the Lolo Canyon, turning right at the Don Tripp
Truck Stop and heading south for Wisdom where the white man
killed his wife. Instead, I think of that drunk afternoon,
still embarrassing, when you, Kittredge and I verbally
shot up the Lolo Tavern. I won't go to the P.O. here
for fear I'll see our photos on the wall. Even worse,
to find out what we're wanted for, to find a halfhearted
offer of a flimsy reward. The Lolo vigilantes
wouldn't recognize me now, not nearly so heavy,
sober as a sloth and given to civility. Still, I drive by
the tavern with my head down. I see you are teaching
with Tate, Cuomo and Fetler. Give Jim and George my best.
Don't know Fetler, but he's a fine writer. Went icefishing
saturday with Yates, Kittredge and our Indian poet friend.
No luck, as Welch says. Cold though. Jesus. The others lushed
it up in Perma. The Dixon Bar is off personal limits
since they misread our *New Yorker* poems and found them
derogating, not the acts of love we meant, not necessarily
for them, but all men and the degraded human condition
we knew long before we heard of Dixon. Why name a town
Wisdom? Why not because an Indian wept once over
the body of his wife, each tear a ton of resolve to make
the trek that will always fail, even if you cross the border
into Canada, and will always be worth while though it ends
a few miles short of your imagined goal, with you erect
in surrender, wind from the soar of ancient horses
blowing your hair, and your words, your words: "I
will fight no more forever" leaving the victorious bent
and forgotten, cheap in their success. Across this nation,

24

dying from faith in progress, I send you and Chris
and the baby a wordy kiss. I will write some more forever
though only poetry and therefore always failure. Dick.

Letter to Peterson from the Pike Place Market

Dear Bob: I'll be damned. The good, oh so utterly sweet
people of Seattle voted to keep the market as is.
I wish I could write tender lines. The way I feel
I could call to gulls in gull language, or name all fish
at a glance the way Wagoner can birds. I'm eating lunch
alone in the Athenian, staring across Puget Sound
to the islands, the blue white Olympics beyond
the islands and the sky beyond them, a sky I know
is reflecting the blue of the ocean. And commerce seems right,
the ships arriving from every nation, the cries of vendors
outside that leak in. Sol Aman the fish man looks good,
and Joe, the Calabrian. The taverns are as usual,
unpretentious, run down, human, and tiers of produce
gleam like Kid Ory's trombone. Today, I am certain,
for all my terrible mistakes I did the right thing
to love places and scenes in my innocent way and to spend
my life writing poems, to receive like a woman
the world in its enduring decay and to tell
that world like a man that I am not afraid to weep
at the sadness, the ongoing day that is draining our life
and is life. Sorry. Got carried away. But you know, Bob, how
in the smoky recess of bars all over the world, a man
will suddenly dance because music, a juke box, a Greek
taverna band, moves him and how when he dances we
applaud and cry go. That's nobility of blood, a recognition
by those who matter that in special moments
we are together facing the brute descent of the sun
and that cold brittle star we know already burned out.
Hell, that's enough. Wish you were here in the market
helping me track down the moment for some euphoric jolt.
The barbecued crab is excellent. Much love. Dick.

26

Letter to Stafford from Polson

Dear Bill: We don't know the new heavy kind of wolf
killing calves, but we've seen it and it's anything but gray.
We have formed a new heavy kind of posse
and we're fanning the Mission range for unique tracks.
The new wolf is full of tricks. For instance, yesterday
he sat all afternoon in a bar disguised as a trout
and none of us caught on. He's a wily one.
He even went home drunk and of course weaving slow,
passed two cars of cops and the Union '76
the usually sharp reliable and somewhat sly one runs.
I guess we're not observant. Aside from the wolf
things go well. This is where you may recall you stood
looking at Flathead Lake and uttered a Stafford line.
Impressed by the expanse you said something about going
on and on. And that's exactly what we've done.
We have a new club called the South Shore Inn,
fair food, good drinks and a panoramic view
of the mountains and lake. Also a couple of posh motels
have been added, a new supermarket and in progress
a mooring harbor for yachts. I personally think
the wolf wants to be one of us, to give up killing
and hiding, the blue cold of the mountains, the cave
where he must live alone. I think he wants to come down
and be a citizen, swim, troll all summer for Mackinaws
and in autumn snag salmon. I have to close now.
The head of the posse just called and two more calves
with throats cut were found this morning one mile south
of the garbage dump. Our chief said this time
we'll get him. This time we plan to follow his howl
all the way to the source, even if it means scaling cliffs
and beating our way through snow. Why does he do it?

He doesn't eat what he kills. I hope we find out. I hope
he breaks and spills all the secrets of his world.
By the way, it turns out he's green with red diagonal stripes
and jitters in wind like a flag. Take care, Bill. Dick.

In Your Small Dream

A small town slanted on a slight hill
in barren land. First building you see:
red brick with oriental trim. You say,
"A unique building," and the road forks
into three. Road left, brief with old men
leaning on brick walls. They frown the sun away.
Middle road, oblique and long. Same red brick
buildings but without the trim. Same drab
roasting buildings. Young men and cafes.
You call it Main Street. The third road
you never see. You walk up Main Street.
You are hungry. You take this opportunity
to eat. You have no money. They throw you out.
You return to the brief street. You ask old men
"Where's the unique building?" They frown
and turn away. You say, "I am a friend."
You know wind will level this town.
You say, "Get out. The wind is on its way."
The old men frown. The day darkens. You look
hard for the third road. You ask a giant, "Where?"
The giant glowers, "The third road is severe."
You run and run. You cannot leave the town.

Letter to Hill from St. Ignatius

Dear Bobbi: God, it's cold. Unpredicted, of course, by forecast,
snow and bitter air drove in from Canada while we, some
students and I, were planning a weekend fishing trip
to Rainbow Lake where, just last week, five of us in four
hours took 44 trout. For all I know that lake is frozen tight,
the trout dormant under the ice for the next five months.
We are shut down. This is a quiet town on the Flathead
Reservation, the staggering Mission Range just beyond,
the mission itself of local historical fame. A priest
some 80 years back designed a ceremony for Good
Friday, Indian-Catholic, complete with Flathead chants
in dialect. It's lovely. This early sudden cold I think
of it, how it reminds me of simple times that no doubt
never were, the unified view of man, all that. I wept
the first time I saw it, the beleaguered Indians wailing
the priest to Stations of the Cross. The pall bearers bearing Christ
outside around fires and crying the weird tongue stark
through the night. Bobbi, I don't mind those real old days broke down.
We had (still have) too many questions. You've known embittering winds
in Green Bay and you are not bitter for all the license
they gave. I resent you once told me how I'd never know
what being Indian was like. All poets do. Including
the blacks. It is knowing whatever bond we find we find
in strange tongues. You won't believe this but after my grim years
alone, a woman who loves me has come along. And she
chants when she talks in the strangest of tongues, the human.
I take her in my arms and don't feel strange. She is tall
and she curls in bed like a cat. And so, like Indians,
I chant the old days back to life and she chants me alive.
It's snowing, Bobbi. The flakes seem heavy and they fall hard
as hail. I claim they ring like bells. And sure enough the far

cathedral complements my claim. Chant to me in your poems
of our loss and let the poem itself be our gain. You're gaining
the hurt world worth having. Friend, let me be Indian. Dick.

Letter to Wagoner from Port Townsend

Dear Dave: Rain five days and I love it. A relief
from sandy arroyos, buzzards and buttes, and a growing season
consisting strictly of June. Here, the grass explodes and trees
rage black green deep as the distance they rage in. I suppose
all said, this is my soul, the salmon rolling in the strait
and salt air loaded with cream for our breathing.
And around the bend a way, Dungeness Spit. I don't need
any guide but the one I've got, the one you threw the world
like a kiss of wind ending hot summer, though of course
I am seldom called lover these days and in bad moments
when I walk the beach I claim the crabs complain. Aside
from those momentary failures I am soaring, looping the loop
over blackfish schools and millions of candlefish darting
in and out of glint. I think because the sea continually
divides the world into dark and gleam, the northwest sky
relieves us from the pressure of always choosing by being
usually gray, but of course that's only theory. No real
accounting for calm. The stable chunky ferry is leaving
for Keystone. Perch curve around the pilings oblivious in
their bulk to porgies and the starfish napping tight to barnacles.
They all remind me of Kenny, a boy I fished with from the pier
at Seola. When we got older I saw he was subnormal and I saw
the space between us grow, and finally we saw each other
in passing in White Center and didn't speak. We don't take
others by the hand and say: we are called people. The power
to make us better is limited even in the democratic sea.
Discovery of cancer, a broken back, our inability to pass
our final exam—I guess the rain is finally getting me down.
What matter? I plan to spend my life dependent on moon
and tide and the tide is coming, creeping over the rocks,

washing the remains of crippled fish back deep to the source,
renewing the driftwood supply and the promise of all night
fires on the beach, stars and dreams of girls, and that's
as rich as I'll ever get. We are called human. C'iao. Dick.

Letter to Bly from La Push

Dear Robert
　　　　Lots of whales cavort and spout
three hundred yards offshore. The danger
of them there, high waves and cold winds mean
we cannot swim. I'm still not in my country
though fishnets dry and hostile eagles scan
our country's enemy, the empty gray.

It's green here, black green mostly, black
against dark sky—all pines are silhouettes.
Even the sun is solid, and red memories
of better runs, of bigger kings, of jacks
that tore the gill nets in their futile drive.
We have to lie or be dishonest to our tears.
Some days I almost know how tall brown wheat
goes gold against dark sky, the storms
that hate our wheat, the thunder
that will come for wheat, evangelistic anger.

My fish is trout. I hear the long jawed pike
can smile you dead when hooked. My symptoms
never die. I've been away ten years, and spray
has killed four houses I remember and the church.
Birds are still fanatic. The shore is raw.
That last rock fist: the void still makes it stick.
The whales are closer and in colder wind
I send warm regards as always,
　　　　　　　　　　　　　Dick

In Your Blue Dream

You are fishing a lake but so far no fish.
The other men fishing are old. They nod approval
of your rod, limber and green. One yells advice
over the lake: develop the eyes of an osprey.
The sun goes down. You row to the shore.
A warden is there. He arrests you. He says
your bait is illegal, live meat. The old men
pay your bail. You sweat when the girl counts the money.
The sky fills with fish hawks each with a trout
in his beak. The streets fill with men enroute home.
You lose your sense of time. You ask the men,
all young, is this afternoon? They don't answer.
You run from man to man asking the time.
You forget your address. You knock on a door.
A luscious blonde tells you you have the wrong town.
You run through the swamp. The town ahead
glitters warm in the dark. You yell at the town,
where is my home? A mob of men with bloodhounds
is back of you somewhere. You hear them. You rush
for the lights. You are in the streets dirty in rags.
The people are elegant, dressed for the clubs.
You show them your key. They answer firmly,
you have the wrong country. Go north. You sob
in the streets. You say, this, this is my land.
The streetlamps dim. A cop says, go home.
When the posse of women find you in the desert
you are terribly ashamed. You babble on and on.
They point at you and laugh. One says, you look good
bleaching, good for a weathered skeleton.

Letter to Libbey from St. Regis

Dear Liz: Here's where I degraded myself for the last time
in front of a clerk, in the gift shop fingering copper
and begging one warped triggering response. Since then
I've been stable, lonely as this town, the solitary river
moving north. I never stop here on my way to Coeur d'Alene.
I pass through hoping 50 years of shame will ripen
into centuries and all men understand. A feeble hope.
Even now I see their grins. I look away at mountains
and I pray all distance widens and I grow old soon. You know,
reach that age where no one wonders why I can't get women.
The worst thing is, I burn alive each day. A letter comes
from some ex-lover and I burn. I tell others she
is coming back to town and they say good, then things may start
again, and I say yes, and inside I am screaming "save me"
and she never comes. I went back to the petty compensations,
writing poems to girls like this one, hoping to imply
a soul worth having, hoping old timidities returned
are temporary and the sun will win. On good days, this
is just a town and I am just a lonely man, no worse
than the others in the bar, watching their lives thin down
to moments they remember in the mirror and those half
dozen friends you make in life who matter, none of them
after you are young. I remember being laid three times
each morning by a tiger angel and that didn't solve
a thing. I went limp to work, feeling like a man, but hell.
I was the same one. And the demons, when they came,
wore the same demonic green they wear in Ireland.
Once, I stopped in Italy, the land no longer torn
by war and wholesale poverty, some village in the south
for coffee. I wowed them joking in bad Italian
and they yelled "ritorni" when I drove away. That's the day

I must remember as the distance widens and I grow old,
not too rapidly. I am dating a 19-year-old lovely
and things slip into place, days I find worth having,
stops I find worth making, flashing some of the old charm
at the waitress and murmuring "ritorno" as I drive away.
And you? How are you doing? Wherever in the world. Rain
has washed grass vivid where we threw up on the lawn, and bars
we hid in have improved the lighting. Next time through
to Coeur d'Alene, I'll stop here more than just to mail a letter.
I'll send you copper, a pendant or a ring. And I'll joke
the clerk to roaring. I plan more poems like this one, poems
to girls, to tiger angels better dawns provide. The dark
that matters is the last one. Autumn's spreading like the best joke
ever told. And I send this with my best laugh, as always. Dick.

Letter to Logan from Milltown

Dear John: This a Dear John letter from booze.
With you, liver. With me, bleeding ulcer. The results
are the horrific same: as drunks we're done. Christ,
John, what a loss to those underground political
movements that count, the Degradationists,
the Dipsomaniacists, and that force gaining momentum
all over the world, the Deteriorationists. I hope
you know how sad this is. Once I quit drinking it was clear
to others, including our chairman (who incidentally
also had to quit drinking), that less 40 pounds
I look resolute and strong and on the surface appear
efficient. Try this for obscene development: they made me
director of creative writing. Better I'd gone on bleeding
getting whiter and whiter and finally blending
into the snow to be found next spring, a tragedy
that surely would increase my poetic reputation.
POET FOUND IN THAW   SNOWS CLAIM MISSOULA BARD
I'm in Milltown. You remember that bar, that beautiful bar
run by Harold Herndon where I pissed five years away
but pleasantly. And now I can't go in for fear
I'll fall sobbing to the floor. God, the ghosts in there.
The poems. Those honest people from the woods and mill.
What a relief that was from school, from that smelly
student-teacher crap and those dreary committees
where people actually say "considering the lateness
of the hour." Bad times too. That depressing summer
of '66 and that woman going—I've talked too often
about that. Now no bourbon to dissolve the tension,
to find self-love in blurred fantasies, to find the charm
to ask a woman home. What happens to us, John?
We are older than our scars. We have outlasted and survived

38

our wars and it turns out we're not as bad as we thought.
And that's really sad. But as a funny painter said
at a bash in Portland, and I thought of you then,
give Mother Cabrini another Martini. But not ever again
you and me. Piss on sobriety, and take care. Dick.

In Your Hot Dream

You are alone on a desert. Hot blasting sand
peppers your face. Your horses are lost. Food
and water are low. You protest the construction
of a furnace. "My argument," you explain,
"is no living room." Speed boats race on a lake.
Other boats, old ones with sails, are burning.
You yell at horses: "Put out the fires." A horse yells
"This is my gear." You find a long stretch of beach,
cool wind and no people. You build a pyre
of driftwood and light it. The flame climbs miles
into the sky. You heap more wood. The flame licks
at stars. You dance the sand in hot glare
and sing an old song: Let The Rest Of The World Go By.
You cry and sweat. The ocean is flaming. The tide
is out of control. Old boats come to your rescue.
Their sails are full. Girls are blowing cold trumpets.

Letter to Gale from Ovando

Dear Vi: You were great at the Roethke festival this summer
in Portland. I love your phrase "and birds move on" because here
that's exactly what they do. It's far better to say
than "fly away" because that indicates they might have stayed
while "move on" says they're vagabond and starved. I'm hungry when
I'm here. It looks anytime like sunday with John Wayne in church,
leaving me helpless, waiting for the villains to ride in.
I only stop here on my way to fish, Brown's lake, or Cooper's,
to feel a part of the west, the brutal part we wave goodbye to
gladly and the honest part we hate to lose, those right days
when we helped each other and were uniformly poor.
How scattered we become. How wrong we end finally alone,
seeing each other seldom, hearing the wind in our teeth.
Roethke himself knew and hated to know the lonely roads
we take to poems. Miriam Patchen was right in her speech
in Portland: it's a one man route and sad. No help. No friend
along the way, standing beside the road with trillium.
And Dickey was right in *Playboy*, that part about the mind
becoming the monster and the monstrous ways we feed it
and it grows. My monster's desolate and kind. And in my
desolate home, the wind leaks in on sundays and finally
for all the gloom, I, not John Wayne, put the villains away
to rest, mark the headstones "no one" and start another poem.
Listen to yourself, Vi: "Lakes change, trees rot and birds move on."
And listen to ourselves move on, each on the road he built
one young summer while the world was having fun. Lakes change.
Trees rot. Roads harden. Whatever road, it was the blind one
and the only. Poems are birds we loved who moved on and remain.
Think of poems as arms and know from this town I am writing
whatever words might find a road across the mountains. Dick.

Letter to Welch from Browning

Dear Jim: This is as far as I ever chased a girl.
She's worth it, but she isn't here. Man, it's a grim pull
from Missoula in a car. Had a haircut in Augusta,
a drink in Choteau, Bynum and Depuyer. I wanted to arrive
well groomed and confident. I'm in a cheap motel,
the walls are beveled board and painted a faint green
that reminds me somehow of the '30s and a cabin
on Lake Meridian. I spent this night, the only white
in the Napi Tavern where the woman tending bar
told me she's your aunt. A scene of raw despair. Indians
sleeping on the filthy floor. Men with brains scrambled in wine.
A man who sobbed all night, who tried in strangled desperation
to articulate the reason. And the bitterest woman I've seen
since the Depression. Of course. The '30s never ended here.
They started. In the '80s. Some braves took turns apologizing
for a poor demented derelict who stole my beer
and bummed me twice for a quarter. One gave me fishing tips
for a lake on the reservation. What a sharp description.
I could see it as he talked. Grass banks that roll into the water.
No trees. Surrounding land as open as the lake. I thanked him
like I'd never thank a white. And I thank a lot of things
because tomorrow I'll be pulling out. When my car points south
I hope a waltz by Strauss is on the radio, the day is sunny
and the clouds so vivid in their forms I'll have the urge
to give them names. I'll never see you quite the same. Your words
will ring like always on the page, but when drunk you shrug
away the world, our petty, gnawing bugs, degrees and grades
and money, even sometimes love, I'll simply nod and pour.
I hope I find that girl. I plan to touch her in such ways,
tender and direct until she reaches for me every morning

out of instinct. She's up here, when she's here, doing social work.
I'll probably never find her. And while I'm at it, the food
in Browning is not good. Take care, Chief Boiling Whiskey. Dick.

In Your Racing Dream

You hitch a ride with a cyclist. You sit in back
and hold on. He's leading in a race. With you
on the cycle he slows down and others pass.
You say to him, "Faster. You'll lose." He says
"I'm thinking of food." You drift a sleepy canal
on a barge, warm horses on the bank, sweep
of grass to trees the wind and light bend
far off in warm air. The water barely moves.
It will take months to cruise home. You snarl
at a horse, "I'm running out of time."
The cyclist goes by. He yells, "I'm winning."
You try to yell "Wait" but choke. He goes on.
You are mayor of a town. The people bring
you their problems. You give advice from
your window. You cannot remember
the canal. You ask, "How did I get here?"
Someone calls you to dinner. You try
and try to remember the cylist's name.

Letter to Snyder from Montana

Dear Gary: As soon as you'd gone winter snapped shut again
on Missoula. Right now snow from the east and last night
cold enough to arrest the melting of ice. My favorite
bouncer, wind, stopped throwing clouds out of the joint for being
too gloomy. In short, you're gone and we've gone back to being
a small dreary city. Some of your grace hangs on. I still
have a date with that round pink girl. For her I have evil plans.
I am rubbing my hands like a monster. I am planning trips
to remote lakes in spring. I know it's not modern to think
of seduction as evil, but damn it that makes it more fun
and the more fun it is the more often I'll do it, I hope.
Students still buzz about your reading. Those who had turned you
into a god were happy to find you human. I should
have warned them. Should have warned all western Montana,
a warm force is coming. Snows will run off. The rivers
will scream and crack their banks. Winter will take a breather.
Speaking of love being fun, you never in your remarks
mentioned those two-minute male orgasms perfected
in India by, if I have it right, mystics. Why not?
Nor did you bring up those ancient Chinese techniques
of tortuous titillation. Remember, forests and land
(for me especially, fish) are not all that's worth saving.
There's also loving. Shit. Why tell you? You preserve that
every day without trying. But of course you're not here.
Last night, 20 below. A mass of tall arctic air
stands over us like a cruel father, though the weather now
is really a mother and this mother may go on forever.
What it needs, what we need, I, is another visit
from Snyder. For that, the glaciers are waiting, and bears
(for you especially, fish) and the green flaring pageant
of sky mating with hills. This letter was found wadded up
in a bum in the tundra who sends his warmest regards. Dick.

Letter to Scanlon from Whitehall

Dear Dennice: I'm this close but the pass is tough this year.
I'm stranded by this rotten winter. My car is ailing
and the local mechanic doesn't know what he's doing
or he does but never learned clear phrasing. It will take
four hours or a week. An odd town. A friendly waitress
says the main drag is the old road so I must have been here
but I don't remember. It looks like several towns
in Montana. Columbus, for one. Even, a little, like the edge
of Billings. You know. On one side, stores, cafes, a movie
theatre you feel certain no one attends. And across
the street, the railroad station. Most of all, that desolate
feeling you get, young hunger, on a gray sunday afternoon,
when you survive only because the desolation feeds
your dying, a dream of living alone on the edge
of a definite place, a desert or the final house in town
with no threat of expansion, or on the edge of a canyon,
coyotes prowling below and a wind that never dies. Girl,
you wouldn't believe the people who live alone, preparing
themselves daily for dying, planning their expenditures
to the penny so just when they die their money is gone
and the county must bury them, a final revenge on a world
that says work is good, plan for the future. They did. And dear
Dennice, bring their laughing bones no flowers. Pay them the honor
of ignoring their graves, the standard bird authorities
chip on stones, a magpie designed by the same man
you always see in towns like this, sitting in the station,
knowing the trains don't run. The soup in the cafe I was lucky
enough to pick of the available three, turned out thick
tomato macaroni, and the chicken salad sandwich, yum.
The mechanic says my car is done. He says, if I understand,
it's ready and no charge. He says, if I understand, he

just wants to be friendly and it wasn't anything really wrong.
Homestake grade is sanded. I may even beat this letter
to your home. It's saturday and I suppose there's a dance
somewhere in Butte tonight. Would you please consider?
Would you come? I hope it's one of those virtuoso bands,
you know, songs from all the generations, jazz, swing, rock.
And a big crowd. Girls in mini minis, tighter than skin
over their behinds, and a friendly bar, a table where
we can talk. Think about it. Say yes. Be nice. Love. Dick.

Letter to Wright from Gooseprairie

Dear Jim: The Bedfords are not to be found. Maybe
they've moved or I've seen them and didn't know it.
I remember most things different. The Bumping River
years ago seemed faster, seemed to play by lovers
on the bank with sumptuous singing, and the trout
seemed bigger too. The world seemed more in motion then.
Clouds pranced the way elk prance and jumped the way
native cutthroat do when hooked. And people seemed uglier,
more like the Bedfords were and probably aren't anymore
and more like people in war. I'm using too many r's.
Our wives are gone too. Mine's remarried. You're married
again, to an unclassified gem. Today, the clouds seem
to move over the meadows the way life seems in retrospect
to have drifted on a pre-set course, uninterrupted
by jolts, fights, sudden changes of direction. Naturally,
an illusion. But then, Jim, time comes to take a rest
the way it comes to take a piss, and to forget the uglies
and cruels, the damage a wrong cloud does. For example,
15 years ago if I had lost a four pound Dolly
after a long struggle I'd have slammed my rod
on the ground. Now, just minutes ago I stopped fishing
because the two trout in my bag are all I can eat.
I rented the same cabin we stayed in then, too big,
I agreed with the owner, for a single, but I have the money
and can pay for the past. I hope I always meet the cost
the way old clouds face doom. Meanwhile, sweet dreams. Dick.

In Your Wild Dream

You are fishing but have walked away from your rod.
Your rod bends and flies into the lake. You swim
to the rod and start reeling in. A huge fish in on.
A gray fish. Bloated. Dull. You finally land him.
On shore he snarls, a vicious mustard dog.
He wants to kill you. He rages with hate and glares.
A man you don't know is holding him back.
The dog strains at the rope. The man says "a Girl fish,
that's what he's called." You are riding a camel
in Athens. The citizens yell, "We are not Arab. This
is not sand." The camel is a yacht. You cruise
a weird purple river. Girls doze on the bank. One
stands up and waves. You yell, "Where is the town?"
You are alone. Fishing again. You catch nothing.
You dream you are dreaming all this. Around you
beautiful flowers are blooming. You know now
you need nothing to live, food, love or water.
Youg giggle and giggle because you are free.
Birds above you keep flying away.

Letter to Haislip from Hot Springs

Dear John: Great to see your long-coming, well-crafted book
getting good reviews. I'm in a town that for no reason
I can understand, reminds me how time has passed since we
studied under Roethke, Arnold Stein, Jack Mathews and
Jim Hall at Washington. Two of them are gone already.
I think of that this morning and I get sad. This motel
I took for the night, hoping to catch the morning fishing
at Rainbow Lake, is one that survived after most others
went broke when they discovered the hot springs simply didn't
work. No therapeutic value. None of that. The old climbed
up out the steaming water still old. The cripples still limped
after three weeks of soaking. I'm a little lame myself
these days. Bad hip from a childhood accident. Skeletal
problems show up as we enter middle age. Our bones
settle in and start to complain about some damn thing that
happened years ago and we barely noticed it then.
Who thought 25 years ago we'd both be directors
of Creative Writing, you at Oregon, me here at
Montana, fishing alone in the' Flathead wind, in lakes
turned silver by sky, my memories so firm, my notion
of what time does to men so secure I wish I'd learned to
write novels. Now I can understand the mind that lets Sam
wander off to Peru on page 29 and come back
twenty years later in the final chapter, a nazi.
I know why I always feel sad when I finish a novel.
Sometimes cry at just the idea that so much has happened.
But then, I'm simply a slob. This is no town for young men.
It sets back off the highway two miles and the streets stand bare.
When I drive in, I feel I'm an intrusion. When I leave,
I feel I'm deserting my past. I feel the same sadness
I feel at the end of a novel. A terrible lot has happened

50

and is done. Do you see it happening to students?
I do and say nothing, and want to say when some young poet
comes angry to my office: you too will grow calm. You too
will see your rage suffer from skeletal weakness you picked
up when young, will come to know the hot springs don't work, and love
empty roads, love being the only man casting into
a lake turned silver by sky. But then, maybe he won't,
no matter. The morning is clear. I plan to grab breakfast
at the empty cafe, then head to the lake, my Buick
purring under the hood as Stafford would say. And I plan
to enjoy life going by despite my slight limp. Best. Dick.

Letter to Mayo from Missoula

Dear Ed: I get the sad news from Des Moines no doubt not sad
for you, that you're hanging it up. That's our loss, everyone
in this game who's teaching poems and ways to write them. You bailed
me out of a classroom jam several times in Portland
at Lewis and Clark that spring, phrasing what I should have said,
clear as Indian sky. But then you have an advantage
over me: you know poetry. I never could read Milton
even in school when I had to. I could recognize Donne
was good but never quite understood him. I suppose I've always
depended on men like you to set it all straight after
I've taught some poet wrong. Ed, I have two retirement
fantasies. One, I walk out of the building the last time
alone, no one saying goodbye. The lights are off. The hall
is dim with winter afternoon. Somehow the retirement
plan got fouled up in the computer and I have no
money to live on (Social Security was voted out
two years before by the new progressive Republican
party). I walk alone in the raw gray air that stings me
cold, to my shack on the river where I sit and wait
to die. No one comes to see me. Finally, I go mad
and am taken away to a home. Two, the speeches ring
in the sunlight. All my students, twenty-five years of them
cheer me as I rise to accept their acclaim. Some of them
are famous poets and they stand up and say, "It's all because
of him," pointing to me. I sob like Mr. Chips and their
applause booms through my tears. I walk alone down the campus,
their voices yelling my name behind me. I am crying
in the car (new Lincoln) and my wife (28, lovely)
comforts me as we speed to our vine and moss covered home
on the lake where I plan to write an even more brilliant
book than my last one, "Me and John Keats" which won the NBA,

52

Pulitzer, APR, Shelley, Bollingen and numerous
other awards and made me a solid contender for
the Nobel. I fear, Ed, neither will do for you, mainly
because you don't take to bullshit kindly. O.K. then this,
I want to retire kind and hardheaded as you, to know
not once did I leave the art, not once did I fail to accept
the new, not once did I forget that seminal coursing
of sound in poems and that lines are really the veins of men
whether men know it or not. And if the saying of it
is, as Stafford says, a lonely thing, it is also
the gritty. Take the hard road home. That is the road you came on
long ago, without drum or banners, without some poet
trying and failing to praise you from the brush in some damn
fool poem like this one. I guess you get what I mean. I mean
take care now. Leave labor to slaves. Give my best to
Myra and show this letter only to trustworthy friends. Luck. Dick.

Letter to Levertov from Butte

Dear Denise: Long way from, long time since Boulder. I hope
you and Mitch are doing OK. I get rumors. You're in Moscow,
Montreal. Whatever place I hear, it's always one of glamor.
I'm not anywhere glamorous. I'm in a town where children
get hurt early. Degraded by drab homes. Beaten by drunken
parents, by other children. Mitch might understand. It's kind
of a microscopic Brooklyn, if you can imagine Brooklyn
with open pit mines, and more Irish than Jewish. I've heard
from many of the students we had that summer. Even seen
a dozen or so since then. They remember the conference fondly.
So do I. Heard from Herb Gold twice and read now and then
about Isaac Bashevis Singer who seems an enduring diamond.
The mines here are not diamond. Nothing is. What endures
is sadness and long memories of labor wars in the early
part of the century. This is the town where you choose sides
to die on, company or man, and both are losers. Because
so many people died in mines and fights, early in history
man said screw it and the fun began. More bars and whores
per capita than any town in America. You live only
for today. Let me go symbolic for a minute: great birds
cross over you anyplace, here they grin and dive. Dashiell
Hammett based *Red Harvest* here though he called it Personville
and "person" he made sure to tell us was "poison" in the slang.
I have ambiguous feelings coming from a place like this
and having clawed my way away, thanks to a few weak gifts
and psychiatry and the luck of living in a country
where enough money floats to the top for the shipwrecked
to hang on. On one hand, no matter what my salary is
or title, I remain a common laborer, stained by the perpetual
dust from loading flour or coal. I stay humble, inadequate
inside. And my way of knowing how people get hurt, make

54

my (damn this next word) heart go out through the stinking air
into the shacks of Walkerville, to the wife who has turned
forever to the wall, the husband sobbing at the kitchen
table and the unwashed children taking it in and in and in
until they are the wall, the table, even the dog the parents
kill each month when the money's gone. On the other hand,
I know the cruelty of poverty, the embittering ways
love is denied, and food, the mean near-insanity of being
and being deprived, the trivial compensations of each day,
recapturing old years in broadcast tunes you try to recall
in bars, hunched over the beer you can't afford, or bending
to the bad job you're lucky enough to have. How, finally,
hate takes over, hippie, nigger, Indian, anyone you can lump
like garbage in a pit, including women. And I don't want
to be part of it. I want to be what I am, a writer good enough
to teach with you and Gold and Singer, even if only in
some conference leader's imagination. And I want my life
inside to go on long as I do, though I only populate bare
landscape with surrogate suffering, with lame men
crippled by more than disease, and create finally
a simple grief I can deal with, a pain the indigent can find
acceptable. I do go on. Forgive this raving. Give my best
to Mitch and keep plenty for yourself. Your rich friend, Dick.

In Your Dream on the Eve of Success

You are talking to a man named Buss. You knew Buss
when you were a child. In life he tends bar. In your dream
he sells greeting cards but not from back of a counter,
in a famous department store. In life
he was your hero, the star softball pitcher
in your grammar school. Your university president
comes to the door. He is elegantly dressed.
Buss holds open the door for the president.
The president can't get through. You help Buss
hold the door open. The president barely gets by.
He seems weak. He limps. He checks some papers
with some men in the next room. You and Buss
watch him through glass. You tell Buss you are a poet.
You ask Buss about his father. Buss says his dad
lived like a gambler. The president tries to cross
the room. His legs are weak and spastic. He falls
helpless on the floor. Two women rush to his side.
He is calm. He tries to show them the papers.
He starts to choke. A woman puts a tomato
in his mouth to stop his choking. You know
he is dying. You cannot understand his calm.

Letter to Kathy from Wisdom

My dearest Kathy: When I heard your tears and those of your
mother over the phone from Moore, from the farm
I've never seen and see again and again under the most
uncaring of skies, I thought of this town I'm writing from,
where we came lovers years ago to fish. How odd
we seemed to them here, a lovely young girl and a fat
middle 40's man they mistook for father and daughter
before the sucker lights in their eyes flashed on. That was
when we kissed their petty scorn to dust. Now, I eat alone
in the cafe we ate in then, thinking of your demons, the sad
days you've seen, the hospitals, doctors, the agonizing
breakdowns that left you ashamed. All my other letter
poems I've sent to poets. But you, your soft round form
beside me in our bed at Jackson, you were a poet then,
curving lines I love against my groin. Oh, my tenderest
racoon, odd animal from nowhere scratching for a home,
please believe I want to plant whatever poem will grow
inside you like a decent life. And when the wheat you've known
forever sours in the wrong wind and you smell it
dying in those acres where you played, please know
old towns we loved in matter, lovers matter, playmates, toys,
and we take from our lives those days when everything moved,
tree, cloud, water, sun, blue between two clouds, and moon,
days that danced, vibrating days, chance poem. I want one
who's wondrous and kind to you. I want him sensitive
to wheat and how wheat bends in cloud shade without wind.
Kathy, this is the worst time of day, nearing five, gloom
ubiquitous as harm, work shifts changing. And our lives
are on the line. Until we die our lives are on the mend.
I'll drive home when I finish this, over the pass that's closed
to all but a few, that to us was always open, good days

years ago when our bodies were in motion and the road rolled out
below us like our days. Call me again when the tears build
big inside you, because you were my lover and you matter,
because I send this letter with my hope, my warm love. Dick.

Letter to Goldbarth from Big Fork

Dear Albert. This is a wholesome town. Really. Cherries grow
big here and all summer a charming theatre puts on
worthy productions. It is Montana at its best, lake
next to town, lovely mountains close by, and independent
people, friendly, generous, always a discernible touch
of the amateur I like. Nothing slick. Montana is
the rest of America 50 years back. Old barber shops
you walk into and don't have to wait. Barbers who take
a long time cutting your hair to make sure they get in all
the latest gossip. Bars where the owner buys every fifth round,
and you buy one for him now and then. Albert, I love it
despite what some think here reading my poems. The forlorn towns
just hanging on take me back to the 30's where most poems
come from, the warm meaningful gestures we make, the warm ways
we search each other for help in a bewildering world,
a world so terrifyingly big we settle for small
ones here we can control. There's a bitter side, too, a mean
suspicion of anything new, of anyone different
or bright. I hate that. I hate feeling as I become well
known that I'm marked: poet, beware. He has insight.
I don't like being tagged negative because I write hurt
as if my inner life on the page is some outer truth,
when it is only my view, not the last word. When it is
not the world photoed and analyzed, only one felt.
I like best of all in Montana how people who've had
nothing from the beginning, never expected a thing,
accept cruelty, weather and man, as normal and who have felt
the bitter strokes of life's gratuitous lash (oh, poets
catch that one), are cheerful, receptive and kind to the end.
So for all their suspicion and distrust of me, they are
my women, my men. And I, who came from the seacoast,

59

who love the salmon, the damp air of Seattle, finally
have come to call this home. That means, when I say it, I lived
here forever and I knew it first time I saw it nine
years ago. Albert, Big Fork brings out the mountain in me.
And trout help, too. Just now, a stranger drove by and waved.
And I waved back my best wave, Albert. I shouted at him
"hello," and it came back doubled by hills. At you too. Dick.

In Your Big Dream

Though alone, you know just over the hill
the army is ready. You decide, if they come,
you'll say you support their cause. You dwell
in the ruins of a church. A bird you know's
ferocious circles the church. You see him
through the huge gaps in the roof. You pull
the bellrope thinking clang will drive him away.
But will it attract the army? You are free
from gravity. You lift five feet off the ground
and glide. You decide to follow a river
all the way to the sea. People along the way
warn you, a monster's downstream. You walk
the streets of a deserted city. You know
it was deserted recently because the lights
still burn and markets display fresh meat.
If anyone comes, you'll say you're chief of police.
Enemy subs pop up on the sea. They shell
the coast. You wave your hair in surrender.
Only one man comes ashore, a small man.
He refuses your terms. He says it's not your land.
You whine. You beg him to take you prisoner.
Bison stampede the plain. You climb a mountain
leading seven men who look like you. They depend
on you for their safety. You climb higher
and higher until you are alone under a sun
gone pale in altitude. You climb above birds
and clouds. You are home in this atmosphere.

Letter to Birch from Deer Lodge

Dear Michele: Once, according to a native, this town
had a choice: state prison or university, and chose
the former. They didn't want whatever radical
was called in those days students and professors with ideas
messing up their town. Now guards in towers, nothing to do,
keep tabs on the streets, the teens cruising the streets in cars,
and report to parents or police anything amiss.
So the town became the pen. They even built a drive-in
across the street from the wall. Burger D and fries within
the shadow of penance. I think, when I'm here, how silly
prisons are, how, if we tore down the grotesque wall and let
all but a handful out, life would be no different, and how
we imprison people not for crimes but simply because
we don't like them, they are unrefined. Crime is our excuse.
Some poets equate themselves with criminals. That may be
because we share the same desolate loves, the same railroad
spur along the swamp ignites some old feeling of self
inside and when the sky comes gray late afternoon across
the world on sunday, we know we're friendless and the hounds bay
in the distance sniffing for our trail. We are equally cowed
by the official, by men who never clown or smile.
And we, poet and felon, know how certain times are right
for others, wrong for us. We die 4 P.M. on friday
when the fun begins for others. And we are like the teens
of Deer Lodge, always under the censorial eye
of the tower. We find secret ways to play. No one
except poets know what gains we make in isolation.
We create our prison and we earn parole each poem.
Michele, our cell door's open like the dawn. Let's run and run.
The day is windy and alive with fields. Your friend. Dick.

Letter to Oberg from Pony

Dear Arthur: In a country where a wealthy handful
of people tear down anything you could possibly love,
break your affectionate connections with yourself by whim
for profit, would move, if they could make money moving it,
the national capital to Dubuque, have already
torn down Walt Whitman's home, tried, damn their souls,
to wreck the Pike Place Market, and in their slimy leisure
plot to dismantle Miss Liberty and move her one piece
at a time to Las Vegas where, reassembled, she
will be a giant slot machine (pull the right arm please,
the one with the torch), you'd love to pack your things and move here.
This is lovely. This is too great for a poem. The only
way here is by dream. Call it Xanadu or Shangri-La
or Oz. Lovely old homes stand empty because somewhere
in this floundering world, the owners toil and plan to come
back here to die. I hope I die here. I want to spend my
last years on the porch of the blue house next to the charming
park the town built and no one uses, picnic tables ringed
by willows and the soft creek ringing in the grass. I hope
to sit there drinking my past alive and watching seasons
take over the park. This is only to assure you, Art,
that in a nation that is no longer one but only an
amorphous collection of failed dreams, where we have been told
too often by contractors, corporations and prudes that
our lives don't matter, there still is a place where the soul
doesn't recognize laws like gravity, where boys catch trout
and that's important, where girls come laughing down the dirt road
to the forlorn store for candy. I love Pony like I love
maybe fifty poems, the ones I return to again
and again knowing my attention can't destroy what's there.
Give my best to Barbara and take care. Dick.

Letter to Blessing from Missoula

Dear Dick: You know all that pissing and moaning around I've
been doing, feeling unloved, certain I was washed up with
romance for good. That has come to an orgiastic halt.
From nowhere came this great woman. I wasn't looking
even when she was suddenly bang in my life. I mean
bang in all the best ways. Bang. Bang. Richard Blessing. And years
of loneliness faded into some silly past where I
stared moodily out my windows at the grammar school girls
passing each morning and fantasized being young again
but with circumstances better than the first time and with
an even newer than new morality current. To
say nothing of saying to myself over and over
"I am retired from romance. I am a failure at love.
Women don't like me. Lecherous, treacherous, kindless klutz.
Oh, that this too too flabby flesh should grow solid. Do not
go gentle into that defeat. Let us go then, you and I
into the deserts of vast eternity." As you can no doubt
see, things became warped, including my memory of how
certain lines go, and all for the wisest of causes:
self-pity. Do not depend on others for sympathy.
When you need sympathy, you'll find it only in yourself.
Now, I need none but I still defend self-pity. I still
say, if this woman hurts me I'll crawl back to my cave.
The snow doesn't get me down. The solid gray overcast
doesn't make me moody. I don't get irritated by
cold clerks in the markets, or barbers who take too long
trimming my hair. This woman is statuesque and soft
and she loves me, meaning she is at my mercy. Have you
noticed when women love us how vulnerable they are?
How they almost challenge us to test them, to be bastards,
to see how much outrageous shit we can fling their way?

Maybe, that's why we've been ripping them off for centuries,
I don't blame them for bitching, turning to movements, fem lib
or whatever they call it. This time, I'm not saying, prove it,
prove your love by not objecting as I steal your money,
set fire to your hair and break your toes with the boots
I took off a dead German soldier at Tobruk. I am
simply going to prove I'm worthy of her love and I feel
I am, which must mean I love her. Boy, am I becoming
tender, and am I ever certain she will not hurt me.
I'll give her no cause. I accept maybe for the first time
love and I luxuriate in it, a glutton, a trout
who had a hard time finding the spawning ground, who swam time
after time the wrong river and turned back discouraged
to the sea, though at moments the sea was fun. Those sex-crazed
sharks and those undulating anemones, can't beat them
when you've had a few drinks though you wake up diseased and raw,
your gills aching and your fins stiff with remorse. That's enough
metaphor. This morning I feel as masculine as you,
and I regard you as the C. C. Rider of poetry,
criticism and trout. This woman will curve from now on
lovely in poems and streams. Look for her in the quarterlies
and pools. I mean real pools, the ones you come to
with Lisa when you take her on picnics. And take Lisa
on picnics. Give her and her cooking my love. Your friend, Dick.

In Your Dream after Falling in Love

Two cops who are really famous actors
playing cops are arrested and must go
to jail. "Not there," one cries. "We'll be killed."
They enter jail with fear. The other prisoners
gloat and yell, "Look who's here. Let's scrub them
good." They give the cops a bath. The cops protest
but seem to enjoy it. You are relieved. You know
things are all right. You are on a tall building
counting the cars way down in the street.
A man whispers, "They seem to be crawling."
"No. No," you say, "they are bright." A worm
turns on you, a giant, big teeth. He means
to eat you alive. You think quick. You
tell him a joke. He laughs himself sick.
He becomes a gull. He climbs up out
of the world of stale air. He is soaring,
a monster glider, and singing, "I am me."
The cell door opens. Fred Astaire dances
his way past the warden into the country.
The warden applauds. A headline says
prisons are abolished. You feel hurt.
You think you'd like your old cell back.
"No way," the grass murmurs, "no way."
You know you have lots of time to catch
the luxurious ship parked at the pier.

Letter to Gildner from Wallace

Dear Gary: The houses in Wallace are closed after 94 years.
Apparently because those forces of Christian morality,
the Republicans, accused the Governor of coddling sin.
One thing about politicians, they can never be whores,
they're not honest enough. They screw man in ways that only
satisfy themselves. I sit in this last bastion
of honesty left in the land, this town Lana Turner
came from (I'll always love you, Lan) with the five best reasons
to be shut down: Oasis, Sahara, U. and I., Lux
and Luxette. Gary, I'd like to tie the self-proclaimed forces
of morality in chairs and bring in swinging professors
and good librarians to lecture on real civilization
for at least ten years, and those who cater to plebiscitic
prudes would have to pass an exam before they could eat.
They wonder why no one believes in the system. What system?
The cynical lean with the wind, whatever one's blowing,
if you'll pardon the vulgar expression. No, Gary, I'll
issue a curse out of my half-Irish past on the hyper
respectable everywhere. May the bluebird of happiness
give you a venereal disease so rare the only known cure
is life in the tundra five hundred miles from a voter,
the only known doctor, a mean polar bear. May the eyes of starved
whores burn through your TV screens as you watch Lawrence Welk.
I'm getting far from my purpose. I wanted to tell you
I still love your poems, then got hung up on people
who won't leave people alone. The most beautiful building
in Wallace is the unused railroad station. The lovely
thing is the way the citizens know in the undergrounds
of their hearts that this isn't right, this sudden shutdown
of what men came to expect long ago when they came down

67

from Lookout Pass and the cold, and the first lights they saw
in the distance warmed them to push on into the waiting
warm arms of release. That's one thing poets best never forget.
May the bluebird of happiness help us remember. Best. Dick.

Note to R. H. from Strongsville

Long day on the road, R. H., and three trips now
I've ended here, in one or another
plastic motel, always the same face at the desk,
polite and pale, and I register
remembering my license number,
leaving what I don't know blank, who I represent.

You're young when you start writing poems, never
dreaming a career that leaves you vodka
and Fresca and some take-out Chinese food,
not good, alone with a grainy TV
watching a Perry Mason replay.
You saw it before but forget the murderer.

I know you're from these parts, some vague wealth
in Cleveland, a manufacturing (clothing I think you said)
fortune, and faced for a long time mournfully,
always in my mind manfully,
close odds on battles for your blood.
Mother at seven to five, a TKO by the eighth.

Mason is trapping the killer. His thundering questions
are closing the trap. An old hack actor is sweating.
Now his big moment: confession.
Now a political program and the other channels
are weak. When I'm alone, no sound, the vodka
and the room begin a roaring of their own.

Call me Weaksville. I'm an R. H. too.
That's not a common bloodtype, just
a way of saying silent roar is where we meet,

usually in print. Better to dream of markets
filled with people, noise, all foods you love to eat
far from Strongsville. They exist.

In Your Good Dream

From this hill they are clear, the people
in pairs emerging from churches, arm
in soft arm. And limb on green limb
the shade oaks lining the streets form
rainproof arches. All day festive tunes
explain your problems are over. You picnic
alone on clean lawn with your legend.
Girls won't make fun of you here.

Storms are spotted far off enough
to plan going home and home has fire.

It's been here forever. Two leisurely grocers
who never compete. At least ten elms
between houses and rapid grass refilling
the wild field for horses. The same mayor
year after year—no one votes anymore—
stocks bass in the ponds and monster trout
in the brook. Anger is outlawed.
The unpleasant get out. Two old policemen
stop children picking too many flowers
in May and give strangers directions.

You know they are happy. Best to stay
on the hill, drowsy witness, hearing
the music, seeing their faces beam
and knowing they marry forever, die late
and are honored in death. A local process,
no patent applied for, cuts name, born date
and died too deep in the headstone to blur.